MALIKA BOUSBAINE

Goal Digger

Master the success mindset and achieve your goals

Copyright © 2024 by Malika Bousbaine

All rights reserved. No part of this publication may be reproduced, stored or transmitted in any form or by any means, electronic, mechanical, photocopying, recording, scanning, or otherwise without written permission from the publisher. It is illegal to copy this book, post it to a website, or distribute it by any other means without permission.

Malika Bousbaine asserts the moral right to be identified as the author of this work.

Malika Bousbaine has no responsibility for the persistence or accuracy of URLs for external or third-party Internet Websites referred to in this publication and does not guarantee that any content on such Websites is, or will remain, accurate or appropriate.

Designations used by companies to distinguish their products are often claimed as trademarks. All brand names and product names used in this book and on its cover are trade names, service marks, trademarks and registered trademarks of their respective owners. The publishers and the book are not associated with any product or vendor mentioned in this book. None of the companies referenced within the book have endorsed the book.

First edition

*This book was professionally typeset on Reedsy.
Find out more at reedsy.com*

*To the dreamers, the doers and the believers
This book is for you.
For every time you have doubted yourself,
For every challenge you have faced,
And for every step you have taken toward your dreams.
May this guide remind you that your potential is limitless,
Your efforts are never in vain,
And the goals you dig for will one day shine brighter than you imagined.
Keep going. You've got this.*

Contents

1. Introduction: The Goal Digger Mindset — 1
2. Chapter 1: The Power of Vision — 4
3. Chapter 2: Breaking Barriers — 9
4. Chapter 3: Goal Setting 101 — 14
5. Chapter 4: Building Winning Habits — 20
6. Chapter 5: Mastering Your Mindset — 27
7. Chapter 6: Mastering Time and Focus — 34
8. Chapter 7: Building Your Dream Team — 42
9. Chapter 8: Celebrating Milestones and Reflecting on Progress — 50
10. Chapter 9: Sustaining Long-Term Success and Creating Your... — 58
11. Chapter 10: The Goal Digger's Road map – Mapping Your... — 65
12. Chapter 11: Embracing the Art of Goal Digger Mastery – From... — 73
13. Conclusion — 81
14. Resources — 86

1

Introduction: The Goal Digger Mindset

What does it really mean to be a 'Goal Digger'? This term, often misunderstood as a playful twist on 'gold digger,' carries a more profound and empowering message. A 'Goal Digger' does not chase material wealth or superficial rewards. Instead, it is someone passionately pursuing their goals with intention, resilience, and purpose. A 'Goal Digger' is bold, ambitious, and unafraid to dream big while taking the necessary steps to bring those dreams to life.

Why Goals Matter

Goals are not just checkpoints on the path of life—they are the blueprint for a transformative and fulfilling existence. Without goals, we drift aimlessly, reacting to circumstances instead of shaping our destiny. Goals give us direction, fuel our ambition, and motivate us when the road gets tough. Whether you want to start a business, write a book, run a marathon, or improve your daily habits, setting and achieving goals is a powerful catalyst for personal growth and transformation.

The Goal Digger's Difference

Being a Goal Digger is not about mindlessly grinding or glorifying the hustle. It is about working smarter, not harder. This means being strategic, intentional, and unapologetic in pursuing what sets your soul on fire. Unlike others who may chase goals out of obligation or comparison, a Goal Digger seeks alignment. They understand that success is not defined by external validation but by achieving goals that resonate deeply with their values and passions.

This book is not just about setting goals but mastering the mindset that helps you achieve them. It is about cultivating the confidence to dream big, the discipline to follow through, and the resilience to bounce back from setbacks. The focus on mindset ensures a comprehensive approach to personal development, equipping you with the tools to navigate the challenges on your journey to success.

What You Will Learn in This Book

You will discover a step-by-step guide to becoming a true Goal Digger in the pages ahead. Whether you are an aspiring entrepreneur, a creative professional, a student, or someone simply looking to level up in life, this book will equip you with:

- **Clarity:** How to identify what you genuinely want and set goals that align with your purpose.
- **Tools:** Proven techniques to stay focused, organized, and productive.
- **Resilience:** Strategies to overcome obstacles and turn failures into stepping stones.
- **Balance:** Insights on how to chase success without sacrificing your health, relationships, or happiness.

INTRODUCTION: THE GOAL DIGGER MINDSET

Who This Book Is For

This book is for anyone ready to dig deep and uncover their potential. Whether starting from nothing or refining your current goals, you will find actionable advice, inspiring stories, and transformative exercises to help you level up. If you have ever felt stuck, overwhelmed, or unsure where to begin, consider this your road map to clarity and success.

Your Journey Starts Here

By picking up this book, you have already taken the first step toward becoming a Goal Digger. You have shown the willingness to invest in yourself, your dreams, and your future. Now, it is time to dig deep, embrace the process, and uncover the treasure that lies within.

Remember, the most valuable gold is not found in the ground—it is in the goals that push you to become the best version of yourself. Let us start digging.

2

Chapter 1: The Power of Vision

Every outstanding achievement begins with a vision. Before goals can take shape, plans can be made, and actions taken, there must be a clear picture of what you want to achieve and why. Vision is the foundation of success—it provides direction, fuels motivation, and gives your efforts meaning. Without vision, even the best plans fall flat.

In this chapter, we will explore the essence of vision, how to discover your unique purpose, and how to craft a compelling vision that pulls you toward your goals with unstoppable energy.

What is a Vision?

Vision is not just a concept; it is deeply personal. It is the ability to see what is and what could be. It is a mental image of your ideal future—a glimpse of the life you want to create or the impact you want to have. Vision serves as your north star, guiding you through challenges, distractions, and moments of doubt. Your values, passions, and aspirations profoundly shape it, making it uniquely yours.

Having a clear vision is not just a motivational cliché; it is a scientifically supported driver of success. Studies show that people with a defined vision and purpose are more likely to achieve their goals because they have clarity and focus.

The Difference Between Dreams and Goals

It is easy to confuse dreams with goals, but they are different. Dreams are broad and inspiring—like "I want to be successful" or "I want to live a happy life." Conversely, goals are specific, measurable, and actionable steps that help bring your dreams to life.
- **Dreams** are the "what." They represent your desires and aspirations.
- **Goals** are the "how." They define the path to turning those dreams into reality.

Vision bridges the gap between the two; the connection keeps you inspired while grounding your efforts in purpose.

Why Vision Matters

When you have a clear vision:
1. **You Gain Clarity:** You know where you are going, which makes it easier to prioritize and make decisions.
2. **You Stay Motivated:** A strong vision is a compass, keeping you focused even when obstacles arise.
3. **You Inspire Others:** A compelling vision can rally support and attract like-minded individuals to your cause.
4. **You Build Resilience:** Knowing your "why" gives you the strength to persevere through setbacks and failures.

Crafting Your Vision

A strong vision is not something you stumble upon—it is something you create. Here are the steps to help you uncover and articulate your vision:

1. **Reflect on Your Passions and Values**
   - What activities make you lose track of time?
   - What causes or ideas ignite your curiosity and energy?
   - What principles do you hold close to your heart?

   Your vision should align with what truly matters to you.

2. **Imagine Your Ideal Life**
   - Close your eyes and picture your future. What does it look like?
   - Where are you? Who are you with? What are you doing?
   - What emotions do you feel in this ideal scenario?

   Allow yourself to dream without limits, and let your imagination run wild.

3. **Identify Your Unique Purpose**
   - What skills, talents, or qualities make you stand out?
   - How can you use those strengths to contribute to the world?
   - What legacy do you want to leave behind?

   A purpose-driven vision is more likely to keep you engaged and fulfilled.

4. **Write It Down**

   A vision is powerful when you put it into words. Write a vivid, detailed description of your ideal future. Use present tense to make it feel genuine (e.g., "I am leading a thriving nonprofit organization that helps undeserved communities access education").

Aligning Your Vision with Your Goals

Once you have crafted your vision, it is time to align it with actionable

goals. Ask yourself:
- What specific steps will help me achieve this vision?
- What skills or resources do I need to acquire?
- How will I measure my progress along the way?

For example, if you want to become a published author, your goals include writing a chapter each month, joining a writing group, or submitting a manuscript to publishers.

Vision Boards: Making Your Vision Tangible

One powerful way to solidify your vision is by creating a vision board. This visual representation of your goals can include images, words, and quotes that inspire you. Place it somewhere you will see daily to keep your dreams at the forefront of your mind.

How to Create a Vision Board:
- Gather magazines, print images, or use digital tools to compile visuals.
- Choose images that resonate with your desired future.
- Arrange them in a way that feels inspiring and meaningful.

Common Challenges and How to Overcome Them
- **Fear of Dreaming Too Big:** Worrying about setting unrealistic expectations is natural. Remember, a bold vision is what sets high achievers apart. Do not be afraid to think big.
- **Lack of Clarity:** Focus on smaller steps if you are unsure about your vision. Try exploring different interests until something clicks. For instance, if you are passionate about art and science, consider a career combining the two, like medical illustration or scientific visualization.
- **Doubt and Impostor Syndrome:** You need not have it all figured

out. Trust that clarity will come as you take action.

The Goal Digger's Mantra

As you move forward, repeat this mantra to yourself:

"I am the architect of my life. My vision guides me, my goals shape me, and my actions define me."

Your vision is the most powerful tool. You must create a life that feels true to who you are. Take the time to dig deep and uncover what truly sets your soul on fire. The next chapter will explore breaking through the barriers holding you back from living out your vision.

3

Chapter 2: Breaking Barriers

Every journey toward success comes with obstacles. Whether it is fear, doubt, or external challenges, these barriers can feel insurmountable if you do not have the tools to overcome them. The difference between those who succeed and those who do not often lies in their ability to break through these barriers and continue forward.

Throughout this chapter, we aim to examine the most common barriers people face, explore their origins, and provide actionable strategies for dismantling them. By the end, you will have the mindset and tools to confront anything that stands between you and your goals.

The Barriers We Face

Barriers to success come in many forms, and while everyone's journey is unique, most challenges fall into three categories:
1. **Internal Barriers:**
  • **Fear of Failure:** Worrying about making mistakes or falling short.
  • **Impostor Syndrome:** Feeling unworthy or incapable of achieving

your goals.

• **Procrastination:** Delaying action due to overwhelm, perfectionism, or lack of motivation.

2. **External Barriers:**

• **Lack of Resources:** Limited access to time, money, education, or support.

• **Toxic Relationships:** Negative or unsupportive people who undermine your confidence.

• **Societal Expectations:** Cultural or societal norms discouraging ambition or nontraditional paths.

3. **Mental Barriers:**

• **Limiting Beliefs:** Thoughts like "I'm not good enough" or "I'll never succeed."

• **Comparison Trap:** Measuring your progress against others instead of your growth.

• **Overthinking:** Getting stuck in analysis paralysis instead of taking action.

Where Barriers Come From

Overcoming these barriers helps to understand their roots. Many internal and mental barriers stem from past experiences, societal conditioning, or fear of the unknown. For example:

• **Fear of Failure** often originates in childhood, where mistakes were punished instead of viewed as learning opportunities.

• **Impostor Syndrome** can arise from perfectionism or growing up in environments where validation is tied to external achievements.

• **Limiting Beliefs** are frequently inherited from family, culture, or early experiences that taught us to doubt our potential.

By recognizing the origins of these barriers, you can begin to challenge and reframe them.

Strategies to Break Through Barriers

1. Reframe Failure as Growth
- Shift your perspective: Failure is not the opposite of success; it is a step toward it. Every successful person has failed multiple times, learning valuable lessons along the way.
- Action Step: Write down your biggest failure and identify three things you learned from the experience. Reflect on how it made you stronger or wiser.

2. Challenge Your Limiting Beliefs
- Limiting beliefs are just stories you tell yourself. Replace "I can't" with "How can I?" to create new possibilities.
- Action Step: Identify one limiting belief you hold and write a counter statement that reflects a growth mindset. For example:
- Limiting Belief: "I'm too old to start a new career."
- Counter statement: "I bring years of valuable experience to any new opportunity."

3. Overcome Impostor Syndrome
- Remember that everyone starts somewhere; perfection is not the goal, progress is.
- Action Step: Create a "win list" of your accomplishments, big or small, and revisit it whenever doubt creeps in.

4. Act Against Procrastination
- Start small. Procrastination often stems from overwhelm, so break big tasks into bite-sized pieces.
- Action Step: Use the "2-Minute Rule" to get started: Commit to

working on a task for just two minutes. Often, starting is the hardest part, and momentum will follow.

5. Create a Supportive Environment
- Surround yourself with people who uplift and encourage you. Distance yourself from negativity when possible.
- Action Step: Identify one person who supports your goals and schedule a conversation with them to share your vision and seek encouragement.

6. Build Resilience
- Resilience is the ability to bounce back after setbacks. Practice self-compassion and view challenges as temporary.
- Action Step: When you face a setback, ask yourself: "What's one thing I can do right now to move forward?"

7. Stop Comparing Yourself to Others
- Comparison is a thief of joy. Focus on your progress and celebrate your unique journey.
- Action Step: Replace scrolling through social media with journaling about your accomplishments or next steps.

Real-Life Stories of Breaking Barriers

Example 1: J.K. Rowling

Before she became one of the world's best-selling authors, J.K. Rowling faced rejection from 12 publishers and was living in near poverty. Instead of giving up, she used these barriers as fuel to keep going. Her determination turned her dream of writing into the global phenomenon of *Harry Potter*.

Example 2: Oprah Winfrey

Oprah faced numerous barriers early in her life, including poverty, abuse, and discrimination. By refusing to let her circumstances define her, she broke through and became one of the world's most influential and successful women. Her story is a testament to the immense power of resilience and self-belief, which resides within each of us, waiting to be unleashed.

The Goal Digger's Tools for Breaking Barriers

- **Affirmations:** Replace negative self-talk with positive affirmations, such as "I am capable, resourceful, and resilient."
- **Visualization:** Spend a few minutes each day visualizing yourself overcoming challenges and achieving your goals.
- **Accountability:** Share your goals with a trusted friend or mentor who can help you stay on track.
- **Growth Mindset:** Embrace the belief that your abilities can improve with effort and learning.

Your Breakthrough Awaits

Breaking barriers is difficult but possible with the right mindset and strategies. Remember, every obstacle you face is an opportunity to grow stronger and more determined. You build momentum, confidence, and resilience each time you break through.

In the next chapter, we will dive into the art and science of goal setting. With your identified barriers and a commitment to overcoming them, you will be ready to transform your dreams into actionable plans.

4

Chapter 3: Goal Setting 101

Goals are the bridges between your dreams and your reality. They empower you to turn your best vision into a tangible reality. Setting clear, actionable goals is the first step toward taking control and progressing in any area of your life. But goal setting is more than just writing down what you want—crafting a specific, achievable, and adaptable plan for your circumstances, making you feel capable and in control.

In this chapter, you will learn how to set powerful goals, avoid common pitfalls, and create a system that helps you stay focused and motivated. By the end, you will have a road map for turning your ambitions into concrete achievements.

Why Goal Setting is Essential

At its core, goal setting is about intention. When you set a goal, you prioritize your time, energy, and resources toward something meaningful. Here's why goals are essential:

1. **They Provide Clarity:** Goals define success and keep you focused.
2. **They Build Motivation:** Achieving small milestones boosts confidence and momentum.
3. **They Encourage Accountability:** Goals help you measure progress and stay on track.
4. **They Reduce Overwhelm:** A well-structured goal breaks big dreams into manageable steps.

Without goals, it is easy to feel adrift, reacting to life instead of shaping it.

The Anatomy of a Great Goal: SMART Goals

The SMART framework is a proven method for setting practical goals. It ensures that your goals are clear, realistic, and actionable. Let us break it down:

1. **Specific**
   - Define precisely what you want to achieve. Vague goals like "I want to get fit" are more challenging because they lack focus. Instead, try "I want to run a 5K."
2. **Measurable**
   - Attach a metric to your goal so you can track progress. For example, "I want to save $10,000" is measurable, whereas "I want to save money" is not.
3. **Achievable**
   - Set goals that challenge you but remain realistic. Aiming to double your income in six months might be unrealistic but increasing it by 10-20% could be achievable.
4. **Relevant**
   - Ensure your goals align with your larger vision and values. Ask yourself, "Why does this goal matter to me?"

5. **Time-Bound**
• Give your goal a deadline to create urgency. For example, "I want to write a book someday" becomes actionable when reframed as "I will complete my first draft by June 30th."

Example SMART Goal:
"I will lose 15 pounds in 3 months by exercising 4 times a week and eating 1,500 calories daily."

Short-Term, Mid-Term, and Long-Term Goals

To achieve your vision, you need a mix of goals with varying timelines:
1. **Short-Term Goals** (1 day to 3 months):
• These are the immediate steps you can take to build momentum.
• Example: "Finish writing the introduction to my book by Friday."
2. **Mid-Term Goals** (3 months to 1 year):
• These are milestones that move you closer to your long-term goals.
• Example: "Complete the first draft of my book by the end of the year."
3. **Long-Term Goals** (1 year or more):
• These are ambitious goals tied to your larger vision.
• Example: "Publish a bestselling novel within the next 5 years."

By breaking down long-term goals into smaller, actionable steps, you will feel less overwhelmed and more motivated to take action.

Common Goal-Setting Mistakes (and How to Avoid Them)
1. **Setting Unrealistic Goals:**
• Ambition is great, but setting impossible goals can lead to frustration.
• **Solution:** Start with smaller, achievable milestones and build from

there.

   2. **Lack of Specificity:**
   • Vague goals make it hard to take action.
   • **Solution:** Use the SMART framework to clarify your objectives.
   3. **Not Writing Goals Down:**
   • Goals that are not written down are easy to forget.
   • **Solution:** Document your goals and review them regularly.
   4. **Setting Too Many Goals at Once:**
   • Spreading yourself too thin can lead to burnout.
   • **Solution:** Prioritize 2-3 key goals at a time.
   5. **Failing to Adjust Goals:**
   • Life changes, and so should your goals.
   • **Solution:** Regularly review your goals and make adjustments as needed.

Creating Your Goal Road map

A road map helps you break your goals into smaller, actionable steps. Here is how:
   1. **Define Your End Goal:**
   • Start with the big picture. What is your ultimate objective?
   2. **Identify Milestones:**
   • Break your goal into key phases or achievements.
   3. **List Action Steps:**
   • Write down every task needed to reach each milestone.
   4. **Set Deadlines:**
   • Assign a timeline to each step.
   5. **Track Your Progress:**
   • Use a journal, app, or planner to monitor your achievements.

Example:

- **Goal:** Save $5,000 in 6 months.
- **Milestone 1:** Save $1,000 in the first month.
- **Milestone 2:** Save $3,000 by month three.
- **Action Steps:**
- Cut unnecessary expenses by $300/month.
- Take on a side hustle earning $200/month.
- Automate savings of $200 per paycheck.

The Role of Accountability

Accountability is a powerful motivator when it comes to goal achievement. Here is how to stay accountable:
- **Share Your Goals:** Tell a trusted friend, mentor, or coach about your plans.
- **Track Your Progress Publicly:** Share updates on social media or a blog.
- **Join a Community:** Find groups or forums where people are working toward similar goals.
- **Reward Yourself:** Celebrate milestones with meaningful rewards to stay motivated.

Staying Flexible with Your Goals

Life is unpredictable, and sometimes goals need to be adjusted. Flexibility is key to long-term success. Here is how to adapt:
- **Reassess Regularly:** Review your goals monthly or quarterly to ensure they are still relevant.
- **Pivot When Necessary:** Do not be afraid to revise your timeline or approach if circumstances change.
- **Focus on Progress, Not Perfection:** Remember, consistent effort matters more than flawless execution.

Goal Digger's Worksheet: A Step-by-Step Guide

At the end of this chapter, complete this exercise to clarify and refine your goals:

1. **Vision Statement:** Write a one-sentence description of your ultimate vision.
2. **Top 3 Goals:** List your three most important goals.
3. **SMART Breakdown:** Use the SMART framework to refine each goal.
4. **Action Plan:** Outline the first three steps you will take to get started.
5. **Accountability Partner:** Write down who you will share your goals with and how they will hold you accountable.

The First Step is the Hardest

Setting goals is easy—taking action is where the real work begins. But the journey becomes easier when you have a clear plan, a strong sense of purpose, and the right tools to stay on track. Remember, every small step you take brings you closer to your dreams.

In the next chapter, we will explore how to build the skills and habits necessary to maintain momentum and achieve your goals confidently and consistently.

5

Chapter 4: Building Winning Habits

Goals are the destination, but habits are the vehicle that gets you there. Success is not just about taking big leaps; it is about the consistent actions you take every day. Habits form the foundation of your productivity, mindset, and progress. The good news is that anyone can build habits that align with their goals and set them up for success.

This chapter will delve into the empowering science of habits, how they form, and how to create systems that make success inevitable. By the end, you will have the tools to build habits that stick and the confidence to tackle your goals one small step at a time, knowing each step is a significant part of your journey.

What Are Habits and Why Do They Matter?

Habits are automatic behaviors, things you do without thinking. Whether you brush your teeth, check your phone, or make your morning coffee, habits shape your daily life. Over time, these small actions compound to create massive results, either positive or negative.

Why Habits Matter:
1. **They Save Energy:** Habits allow you to perform tasks without expending mental energy on decision-making.
2. **They Shape Identity:** Your habits reinforce how you see yourself (e.g., "I'm the kind of person who works out every day").
3. **They Drive Results:** Consistency, not intensity, is the key to long-term success.

The Habit Loop: How Habits Are Formed

Habits are formed through a cycle known as the **Habit Loop**, which has three components:
1. **Cue:** A trigger that initiates the habit.
For example, feeling stressed.
2. **Routine:** The behavior or action you perform.
For example, eating a snack to relieve stress.
3. **Reward:** The positive reinforcement that encourages the habit.
For instance, snacking makes you feel better, reinforcing the habit loop.

By understanding this, you can intentionally create new habits or break old ones, giving you the power to shape your life how you want it to be.

Creating New Habits: The Science of Behavior Change

Building a new habit can feel challenging, but with the right strategy, it becomes easier. Here is how:

1. Start Small

- Focus on a tiny version of your habit to make it achievable.
- Example: Instead of aiming to run five miles, start with a five-minute walk.

2. Anchor Habits to Existing Routines
- Use an existing habit as a cue for your new one.
- Example: "After I brush my teeth, I'll spend five minutes journaling."

3. Make It Easy
- Reduce friction by simplifying the habit.
- Example: Lay out your workout clothes the night before to make morning exercise easier.

4. Use Positive Reinforcement
- Reward yourself for sticking to your habit.
- Example: Treat yourself to your favorite coffee after a week of workouts.

5. Track Your Progress
- Keep a record of your habit to stay motivated.
- Example: Use a habit tracker app or a calendar to mark off days you succeed.

Breaking Bad Habits

Breaking a bad habit requires disrupting the habit loop. Here is how to do it:

1. Identify Triggers
- Pay attention to the cues that trigger your bad habit.
- Example: Do you snack when bored, tired, or stressed?

2. Replace the Routine
- Swap the undesirable habit with a healthier one.
- Example: Instead of scrolling social media when bored, pick up a book or go for a walk.

3. Change Your Environment
- Remove temptations or make it harder to engage in the habit.
- Example: Keep junk food out of the house if you are trying to eat healthier.

4. Use Accountability
- Share your goal to break the habit with someone who will encourage you.
- Example: Tell a friend about your plan to quit smoking and ask them to check your progress.

5. Be Patient
- Breaking a habit takes time and effort. Be kind to yourself during setbacks and keep going.

Keystone Habits: The Habits That Change Everything

Some habits have a ripple effect, positively influencing multiple areas of your life. These are called **keystone habits.**

Examples of Keystone Habits:
- **Exercise:** Regular physical activity improves energy, focus, and mood.
- **Meal Planning:** Healthy meals lead to better health and time management.
- **Journaling:** Writing down your thoughts fosters self-awareness and emotional clarity.

- **Morning Routines:** Starting your day with intention sets the tone for productivity.

Focusing on keystone habits creates a foundation for other positive behaviors to flourish.

The Power of Systems Over Goals

James Clear, author of *Atomic Habits*, emphasizes that "you don't rise to the level of your goals; you fall to the level of your systems." While goals provide direction, systems ensure consistent progress."

What is a System?

A system is a set of daily habits and routines that support your goals. For example:
- **Goal:** Write a book.
- **System:** Write 500 words every morning before checking your phone.

How to Build a System:
1. **Identify the Outcome You Want:** What is the goal you are working toward?
2. **Break It Down Into Daily Actions:** What small habits will move you closer to that goal?
3. **Focus on Consistency Over Perfection:** Aim to show up every day, even if it is just for five minutes.

Staying Motivated and Overcoming Plateaus

Even with intense habits, you may hit plateaus or lose motivation. Here is how to stay on track:

1. Revisit Your "Why"
• Remind yourself of the deeper purpose behind your habits and goals.

2. Gamify the Process
• Turn your progress into a game by setting challenges or earning rewards.

3. Find an Accountability Partner
• Share your habits with someone who will celebrate your wins and keep you accountable.

4. Mix Things Up
• Introduce variety to avoid boredom.
• Example: If you exercise, try new activities like yoga, hiking, or swimming.

5. Focus on the Long Term
• Remember that minor improvements add up over time. Trust the process.

Habit Stacking: A Practical Tool for Success

Habit stacking is a technique for pairing a new habit with an existing one, making incorporating new behaviors into your routine more manageable. It is a way to piggyback a new habit onto an existing one, so you do not have to rely solely on willpower to make a change.

Formula:

"After [current habit], I will [new habit]."

Examples:

- After I pour my morning coffee, I will read one page of a book.
- After I take off my work shoes, I will do 10 minutes of yoga.
- After brushing my teeth, I will write down one thing for which I am grateful.

The Goal Digger's Daily Habit Blueprint

By the end of this chapter, create your daily habit blueprint:

1. **Morning Routine:**
   - What habits will set you up for success each morning?
   - Example: Meditate for 5 minutes, journal your priorities, and drink a glass of water.
2. **Work Routine:**
   - What habits will help you stay productive and focused during the day?
   - Example: Use the Pomodoro technique for focused work sessions.
3. **Evening Routine:**
   - What habits will help you wind down and prepare for tomorrow?
   - Example: Reflect on the day, plan your next steps, and unplug from screens an hour before bed.

Habits That Last a Lifetime

Habits are the invisible architecture of your life. By mastering the art of habit-building, you can create a life that aligns with your vision and goals. The small, consistent actions you take every day will ultimately define your success.

In the next chapter, we will explore the role of mindset and how cultivating a positive, growth-oriented outlook can supercharge your journey to becoming a Goal Digger.

6

Chapter 5: Mastering Your Mindset

Your mindset is the foundation of everything you achieve. It is the lens through which you view challenges, setbacks, and opportunities. A strong and positive mindset can propel you toward your goals, while a fixed or negative mindset can hold you back. Becoming a *Goal Digger* requires cultivating a mindset that embraces growth, resilience, and unshakable belief in your potential.

This chapter delves into the power of mindset, the science behind it, and actionable strategies to reframe your thinking. By the end of this chapter, you will be equipped to overcome self-doubt, silence negative inner voices, and build the mental toughness needed to thrive on your journey.

What is Mindset?

At its core, mindset is your attitude and beliefs about yourself and the world around you. Carol Dweck, a psychologist and author of *Mindset: The New Psychology of Success*, identifies two main types of mindsets:

1. Fixed Mindset
  • Belief: Your abilities, talents, and intelligence are static and unchangeable.
  • Characteristics:

  • Avoids challenges for fear of failure.
  • Views effort as pointless if success is not guaranteed.
  • Feels threatened by others' success.

2. Growth Mindset
  • Belief: Your abilities and intelligence develop through effort, learning, and persistence.
  • Characteristics:

  • Embraces challenges as opportunities to grow.
  • Sees failure as a stepping stone to success.
  • Finds inspiration in others' achievements.

Embracing a growth mindset as a Goal Digger means seeing every obstacle as a chance to learn and grow, leading to a more fulfilling and successful life.

The Power of Positive Thinking

Remember, your thoughts shape your reality. Focusing on limitations can hinder progress, but a positive mindset can open doors to creativity, solutions, and resilience.

How Positive Thinking Affects Success:

1. **Improved Problem-Solving:** A positive outlook helps you see challenges as puzzles to solve rather than insurmountable problems.
2. **Increased Motivation:** Optimism fuels your drive, even when the journey gets tough.
3. **Better Relationships:** A positive attitude fosters connection and collaboration.
4. **Enhanced Resilience:** Positivity helps you bounce back faster from setbacks.

Common Mindset Roadblocks (and How to Overcome Them)

Even with the best intentions, negative thoughts and limiting beliefs can creep in. Here is how to identify and tackle them:

1. Fear of Failure
- **Challenge:** Worrying about failure can stop you from taking risks.
- **Reframe:** Failure is feedback. Every mistake teaches you what does not work and moves you closer to success.

2. Impostor Syndrome
- **Challenge:** Feeling like you do not deserve success or doubting your abilities.
- **Reframe:** Remind yourself of your achievements and focus on continuous learning. Success is not about perfection—it is about growth.

3. Perfectionism
- **Challenge:** Waiting for everything to be "perfect" before starting.
- **Reframe:** Progress is more important than perfection. Taking imperfect action is better than taking no action at all.

4. Comparison Trap
- **Challenge:** Comparing your journey to others' successes can lead to feelings of inadequacy.
- **Reframe:** Use others' achievements as inspiration, not competition. Focus on your unique path.

Rewiring Your Brain: Neuroplasticity and Mindset

Through neuroplasticity, your brain has an incredible ability to change and adapt. You can train your brain to think more positively, embrace challenges, and develop resilience.

How to Rewire Your Brain:

1. **Gratitude:** One powerful way to rewire your brain is through the practice of gratitude. Focusing on what you have rather than what you lack can shift your mindset towards abundance.
- Example: Write down three things you are grateful for every morning.

2. **Affirmations:** Positive affirmations reinforce empowering beliefs about yourself.
- Example: "I can achieve my goals through hard work and persistence."

3. **Visualization:** Picture yourself achieving your goals in vivid detail, which will prime your brain to work toward them.
- Example: Spend five minutes each day visualizing your success.

4. **Challenge Negative Thoughts:** Whenever a negative thought arises, replace it with a more empowering perspective.

Building Resilience: The Mindset of a Goal Digger

Resilience, the ability to bounce back from adversity, is key to success. A resilient mindset helps you persevere through setbacks and keeps your focus firmly on your goals, instilling in you a sense of determination and persistence.

Strategies for Building Resilience:
1. **Embrace the Learning Process:** Treat every challenge as an opportunity to learn and grow.
2. **Cultivate Optimism:** Look for the unseen benefit under challenging situations.
3. **Develop Emotional Regulation:** Practice mindfulness or meditation to manage stress and maintain focus.
4. **Lean on Your Support System:** Surround yourself with people who uplift and encourage you.

Mindset Shifts for a Goal Digger

1. From "I Can't" to "I Can Learn".
- **Old Mindset:** "I can't do this."
- **New Mindset:** "I may not know how yet, but I can learn and improve."

2. From "This is Too Hard" to "This is a Challenge I Can Overcome".
- **Old Mindset:** "This is too difficult for me."
- **New Mindset:** "I've overcome tough challenges before and can do it again."

3. From "I'm Not Ready" to "I'll Start and Figure It Out".
- **Old Mindset:** "I need everything to be perfect before I start."
- **New Mindset:** "I'll take the first step and adapt as I go."

Creating a Goal Digger Mindset Ritual

A daily ritual can help you cultivate the right mindset and set the tone for your day. Here is a simple framework:

1. **Morning Affirmations:** Start your day with positive self-talk.
   - Example: "I am capable, focused, and ready to achieve my goals."
2. **Visualization Practice:** Spend a few minutes imagining yourself succeeding in your goals.
3. **Gratitude Journal:** Write down three things you are thankful for to foster positivity.
4. **Set Intentions:** Decide on one key focus for the day that aligns with your goals.
5. **End-of-Day Reflection:** Reflect on your wins, lessons, and what you will improve tomorrow.

Mindset Worksheet: Your Personal Reframe Plan

Use this worksheet to reframe negative beliefs and cultivate a growth mindset:

1. **Identify a Limiting Belief:** Write down a thought holding you back.
   - Example: "I'm not smart enough to succeed."
2. **Challenge the Belief:** Ask yourself, "Is this true?" or "What evidence do I have to the contrary?"
3. **Reframe the Belief:** Replace it with a more empowering statement.
   - Example: "I can learn and grow through effort and persistence."
4. **Take Action:** List one step you will take to reinforce the new belief.

Final Thoughts on Mindset Mastery

Your mindset is your greatest asset as a *Goal Digger*. With the correct beliefs and mental habits, you can overcome obstacles, stay motivated, and turn your dreams into reality. Remember, growth is a lifelong process. Every day is an opportunity to strengthen your mindset and move closer to the person you want to become.

In the next chapter, we will explore how to manage time effectively and eliminate distractions so you can stay laser-focused on your goals.

7

Chapter 6: Mastering Time and Focus

Time is one of the most valuable resources you have. Unlike money or energy, you cannot earn more of it. You have 24 hours—1,440 minutes—to spend daily. The key to becoming a true *Goal Digger* is learning to manage your time effectively and focus on what truly matters.

This chapter will teach you how to prioritize goals, eliminate distractions, and create systems that maximize productivity. By the end of this chapter, you will have the tools to take control of your schedule, align your time with your priorities, and stay laser-focused on your most important tasks.

The Time-Mindset Connection

Time management begins with a mindset. Many people fall into one of two traps:

1. **Scarcity Mindset:** Feeling there's "never enough time" and constantly rushing.

2. **Procrastination Mindset:** Believing you will "have more time later" and putting off important tasks.

Both mindsets are limiting. Instead, adopt a **Priority Mindset**, where you view time as a resource you can allocate intentionally.

Understanding Where Your Time Goes

Before you can master your time, you must understand how you spend it. This understanding is a powerful tool, empowering you to take control of your schedule and make intentional choices about how you use your time. It is not about managing time; it is about managing yourself and your activities, and this knowledge puts you firmly in the driver's seat of your life.

Step 1: Track Your Time

Log everything you do, including work, personal tasks, and leisure activities, for a week using a notebook, spreadsheet, or time-tracking app.

Step 2: Analyze the Results

Ask yourself:
- Which activities align with my goals?
- Where am I wasting time?
- Are there low-value tasks I can delegate or eliminate?

The 80/20 Rule: Focus on High-Impact Activities

The **Pareto Principle**, or the 80/20 Rule, states that 80% of your results come from 20% of your efforts. Identify and focus on the tasks that drive the most significant progress toward your goals.

Examples of High-Impact Activities:
- For career growth: Building skills, networking, and creating high-quality work.
- For personal goals: Exercising, journaling, or working on a passion project.
- For relationships: Spending quality time with loved ones.

Eliminating the 80%:

By reducing tasks that do not move the needle, such as excessive meetings, busy work, or mindless social media scrolling, you will free yourself from unnecessary burdens and create space for what truly matters.

Creating a Time Management System

1. The Eisenhower Matrix

This tool helps you prioritize tasks based on urgency and importance. Divide tasks into four quadrants:
1. **Urgent & Important:** Do these immediately.
- Example: Meeting a project deadline.
2. **Important but Not Urgent:** Schedule these for later.
- Example: Planning a long-term goal or learning a new skill.
3. **Urgent but Not Important:** Delegate or minimize these.
- Example: Answering non-essential emails.
4. **Not Urgent & Not Important:** Eliminate these.
- Example: Watching endless TV shows or browsing memes.

2. Time Blocking

Assign specific blocks of time to each task or activity. Treat these blocks as unbreakable appointments with yourself.
- Example:
- 8:00–9:00 AM: Exercise
- 9:30–11:30 AM: Work on a key project
- 12:00–12:30 PM: Lunch and recharge

3. Batch Processing

Group similar tasks together to reduce mental switching and increase efficiency.
- Example: Respond to all emails at once instead of checking your inbox throughout the day.

4. Set Boundaries

Protecting your time is crucial. By learning to say no to commitments that do not align with your priorities, you set boundaries that bring a sense of relief, knowing that you are in control of your time and commitments.

Overcoming Distractions

Distractions are the biggest enemy of focus. Distractions, like your phone buzzing, social media notifications, or an overflowing to-do list, drain your productivity.

Common Distractions and How to Handle Them:
1. **Digital Distractions:**

- Turn off notifications or put your phone on Do Not Disturb.
- Use productivity apps like Freedom or Focus@Will to block distracting websites.

2. **Physical Clutter:**
- Keep your workspace clean and organized to reduce mental clutter.

3. **Interruptions from Others:**
- Politely communicate your focus time to coworkers, family, or friends.

4. **Internal Distractions:**
- Practice mindfulness to quiet your mind and bring your focus back to the task.

The Power of Focus: Deep Work vs. Shallow Work

Productivity expert Cal Newport defines two types of work:

1. **Deep Work:** Focused, high-value tasks that require concentration and skill.
- Example: Writing a report, designing a product, or solving a complex problem.

2. **Shallow Work:** Low-value tasks that are easy to complete but do not contribute much to your goals.
- Example: Responding to routine emails or attending unnecessary meetings.

To maximize your results, spend more time in **deep work** and minimize **shallow work**.

The Goal Digger's Daily Schedule

Here is a sample daily schedule to maximize time and focus:
- **Morning:**

- Set intentions for the day.
- Tackle your most important task (deep work) first.
- **Midday:**
- Take a break to recharge.
- Handle smaller, shallow tasks.
- **Afternoon:**
- Return to a high-priority task or project.
- **Evening:**
- Reflect on your accomplishments.
- Prepare for tomorrow.

Dealing with Procrastination

Even the most disciplined Goal Diggers face procrastination. Here is how to overcome it:

1. Identify the Root Cause
- Is it fear of failure? Lack of clarity? Overwhelm? Understanding the reason can help you address it.

2. Use the 2-Minute Rule
- If a task takes less than two minutes, do it immediately.

3. Break Big Tasks into Smaller Steps
- Start with a manageable piece of the task to build momentum.

4. Set Deadlines
- Self-imposed deadlines create urgency and prevent tasks from dragging on indefinitely.

Staying Accountable

Accountability keeps you on track and ensures you follow through on your plans.

1. Use Accountability Partners
- Share your goals with a friend, mentor, or coach who will check your progress.

2. Leverage Technology
- Use apps like Trello, Todoist, or Notion to organize tasks and track your progress.

3. Reward Yourself
- Celebrate small wins to keep yourself motivated and excited about your progress.

Time and Focus Worksheet

Step 1: Write Down Your Priorities
- What are the top three goals you want to work toward this week?

Step 2: Identify Your High-Impact Tasks
- What tasks will bring you closer to achieving these goals?

Step 3: Schedule Your Day
- Use time blocking or another system to allocate specific time for these tasks.

Step 4: Reflect and Adjust
- At the end of each day, review your progress and tweak your schedule as needed.

Final Thoughts on Time Mastery

Time and focus are the ultimate tools for turning dreams into reality. You can achieve more than you ever thought possible by controlling your schedule, eliminating distractions, and prioritizing what matters most.

In the next chapter, we will explore how to build a network of support and collaboration because even the most driven Goal-Diggers will not succeed alone.

8

Chapter 7: Building Your Dream Team

No *Goal Digger* achieves success in isolation. The most impactful achievements are often the result of collaboration, support, and a strong network of people who believe in your vision. Your 'Dream Team' is not just a professional network—it is a group of individuals who inspire, challenge, and support you in different ways.

Building this Dream Team is a powerful act of empowerment, a testament to your capability and potential.

This chapter explores building meaningful relationships, cultivating a strong support system, and leveraging teamwork to accelerate progress. By the end of this chapter, you will understand how to surround yourself with the right people and create an environment that fosters success.

The Importance of Relationships in Achieving Goals

1. Inspiration and Motivation

CHAPTER 7: BUILDING YOUR DREAM TEAM

The right people inspire you to dream bigger and push through challenges. Being around ambitious, driven individuals can energize you and keep you motivated.

2. Accountability

When you share your goals with others, you are more likely to stay on track. Accountability partners help you remain focused and consistent.

3. Access to Resources and Knowledge

Your network can provide insights, advice, and opportunities that you might not access on your own.

4. Emotional Support

Achieving big goals often comes with setbacks and self-doubt. A supportive circle helps you navigate challenging times.

Identifying Your Dream Team

Your Dream Team can include people from all areas of your life. Consider building a diverse group that fulfills different roles:

1. Mentors
   • **Who They Are:** Individuals with experience and wisdom in your field or interest.
   • **How They Help:** Provide guidance, share lessons from their journey, and help you avoid pitfalls.

2. Accountability Partners

- **Who They Are:** Peers or colleagues with similar goals or ambitions.
- **How They Help:** Check in on your progress and ensure you stay committed to your goals.

3. Cheerleaders
- **Who They Are:** Friends, family, or supporters who believe in you unconditionally.
- **How They Help:** Offer emotional encouragement and celebrate your wins with you.

4. Collaborators
- **Who They Are:** Individuals with complementary skills who can work with you on projects.
- **How They Help:** Share the workload, bring fresh perspectives, and enhance the quality of your work.

5. Connectors
- **Who They Are:** People with extensive networks can introduce you to opportunities or key contacts.
- **How They Help:** Open doors to new partnerships, resources, and ideas.

How to Attract the Right People

1. Be Clear About Your Goals

Finding people who align with your vision is easier when you know what you want. Be specific about your goals and the type of support you are seeking.

2. Add Value First

CHAPTER 7: BUILDING YOUR DREAM TEAM

Before asking for help, look for ways to support or contribute to others. Building strong relationships starts with generosity.

3. Be Authentic

Genuine connections are built on trust and honesty. Be yourself and show genuine interest in others.

4. Show Gratitude

Always express appreciation for the people who support you. Gratitude strengthens relationships and encourages future collaboration.

5. Network Intentionally

Seek out communities, events, and groups where like-minded individuals gather, including professional organizations, online communities, or social events.

Nurturing Relationships

Building a Dream Team is not just about meeting the right people—it is about cultivating lasting relationships.

1. Communicate Regularly

Stay in touch with your network through emails, calls, or casual check-ins. Consistent communication keeps relationships strong.

2. Celebrate Their Success

Show genuine happiness for others' achievements. Success is not a competition but an opportunity to uplift each other. Celebrating others' success strengthens your bond with them and makes you feel part of a larger, supportive community.

3. Be a Source of Support

Offer help or encouragement whenever you can. The more you invest in others, the more they invest in you.

4. Respect Boundaries

Be mindful of people's time and commitments. Strong relationships rely on mutual respect.

The Power of Collaboration

Collaboration multiplies your impact by combining strengths, skills, and ideas. A well-coordinated team can achieve far more than any individual alone.

Benefits of Collaboration:
- **Diverse Perspectives:** Team members bring unique viewpoints and ideas.
- **Shared Workload:** Tasks are shared, reducing stress and increasing efficiency.
- **Increased Innovation:** Collaboration sparks creativity and new solutions.
- **Enhanced Motivation:** Working alongside others keeps you accountable and inspired.

How to Collaborate Effectively:

CHAPTER 7: BUILDING YOUR DREAM TEAM

1. **Define Roles Clearly:** Ensure everyone understands their responsibilities.
2. **Communicate Openly:** Maintain transparency and address issues promptly.
3. **Foster Trust:** Trust is the foundation of any successful collaboration.
4. **Celebrate Team Wins:** Acknowledge the contributions of all team members.

Overcoming Relationship Challenges

Not all relationships will be smooth. Here is how to address common challenges:

1. Managing Conflicts
  • **Solution:** Approach conflicts with empathy and a problem-solving mindset. Focus on finding common ground.

2. Dealing with Toxic Relationships
  • **Solution:** If someone consistently drains your energy or undermines your goals, setting boundaries or distancing yourself is okay.

3. Balancing Give-and-Take
  • **Solution:** Aim for reciprocity. Relationships thrive when there is a balance of support and contribution.

Your Relationship-Building Action Plan
1. **Map Your Current Network:**
   • Write down the people who currently support you.
   • Identify gaps in your network (e.g., a mentor, collaborator, or accountability partner).

2. **Set Relationship Goals:**
• What kind of relationships do you want to build?
• How many new connections will you aim for this month?

3. **Take Action:**
• Attend networking events, reach out to potential mentors, or schedule coffee chats with inspiring individuals.

4. **Follow Up:**
• After meeting someone, send a thank-you note or follow-up message to stay connected.

Dream Team Examples

Example 1: Entrepreneur Building a Business
• Mentor: A successful business owner in a similar industry.
• Collaborator: A graphic designer who creates marketing materials.
• Cheerleader: A best friend who motivates and supports during tough times.
• Accountability Partner: A fellow entrepreneur who checks in weekly.
• Connector: A local investor who introduces them to potential partners.

Example 2: Aspiring Author
• Mentor: A published author offering advice on writing and publishing.
• Collaborator: An editor or writing coach.
• Cheerleader: A sibling who encourages creativity.
• Accountability Partner: A member of a writing group.
• Connector: A literary agent or book club member with industry contacts.

Final Thoughts on Building Your Dream Team

Success is rarely a solo journey. By surrounding yourself with the right people, you create an ecosystem of support, encouragement, and collaboration. Your Dream Team will inspire you to reach new heights and provide the resources to realize your goals.

In the next chapter, we will explore the importance of celebrating milestones and reflecting on your progress to maintain momentum.

9

Chapter 8: Celebrating Milestones and Reflecting on Progress

The path to success is filled with challenges, hard work, and dedication. But pausing and celebrating your victories along the way is equally important. Acknowledging milestones, no matter how big or small, boosts motivation, reinforces positive habits, and reminds you of your progress.

In this chapter, we will explore the importance of celebration, how to track your achievements, and how reflection helps refine your journey. By the end, you will have strategies to savor your successes while maintaining focus on your long-term goals.

Why Celebrate Milestones?

Celebration is a feel-good exercise and a powerful tool for growth and motivation. A moment of joy uplifts your spirit and energizes you for the journey ahead.

CHAPTER 8: CELEBRATING MILESTONES AND REFLECTING ON PROGRESS

1. Builds Momentum

Recognizing small wins propels you forward. Each milestone proves that you can achieve your bigger goals.

2. Boosts Confidence

Celebrating achievements reminds you of your strengths and reinforces your ability to overcome challenges.

3. Prevents Burnout

Acknowledging progress creates a sense of accomplishment, making the journey rewarding rather than exhausting.

4. Reinforces Habits

When you celebrate successes tied to your habits, it encourages you to keep up those behaviors.

Identifying Milestones

Milestones are benchmarks that signify meaningful progress. They can vary depending on the nature of your goal.

Short-Term Goals:
- Completing a chapter of a book you are writing.
- Saving your first $1,000 toward a more significant financial goal.
- Losing the first 5 pounds in your fitness journey.

Long-Term Goals:

- Publishing a book.
- Saving for a house or retirement.
- Completing a marathon or hitting a significant fitness milestone.

Personal Growth Goals:
- Overcoming a fear or stepping out of your comfort zone.
- Mastering a new skill.
- Establishing a consistent routine, such as meditating daily for a month.

Ways to Celebrate Milestones

Celebrations do not have to be extravagant. What matters is recognizing your efforts and rewarding yourself in meaningful ways.

1. Treat Yourself

Reward yourself with something you enjoy, like a nice meal, a day off, or a small gift.

2. Share Your Success

Celebrate with friends, family, or your Dream Team. Sharing your achievements strengthens relationships and inspires others.

3. Document the Moment

Take a photo, write about your achievement, or create a visual representation of your progress, like a journal or scrapbook.

4. Reflect on Your Journey

CHAPTER 8: CELEBRATING MILESTONES AND REFLECTING ON PROGRESS

Consider how far you have come, the challenges you have overcome, and the lessons you have learned.

5. Set a New Goal

Use the momentum of your success to inspire and aim for the next milestone. Setting new goals keeps the fire of inspiration burning.

Reflection: The Key to Sustainable Growth

Reflection is looking back on your progress to learn, grow, and improve. It is a powerful tool that empowers you, providing clarity and direction for the future.

Benefits of Reflection:
- **Identifies What's Working:** Helps you focus on practical strategies.
- **Reveals Areas for Improvement:** Highlights challenges and obstacles you can address.
- **Strengthens Commitment:** Reinforces your "why" and deepens your connection to your goals.

How to Reflect Effectively

1. Schedule Regular Check-Ins

Set aside time weekly, monthly, or quarterly to review your progress.

2. Ask Reflective Questions
- What milestones have I achieved?
- What challenges did I face, and how did I overcome them?
- What lessons have I learned?

- How have my actions aligned with my goals?
- What can I do differently to move forward?

3. Use a Journal

Writing your reflections helps solidify your insights and records your journey.

4. Seek Feedback

Ask trusted mentors, peers, or collaborators for their perspectives on your progress and areas for growth.

Overcoming the Fear of Self-Celebration

Many people struggle to celebrate their achievements because they feel self-indulgent or worry it might seem arrogant. Here is why you should embrace self-celebration:

1. It is Not About Bragging

Celebration is a personal acknowledgment of your hard work. It is not about seeking validation from others.

2. It Creates Positive Energy

Recognizing your successes generates motivation and happiness, which fuel further progress.

3. It Honors Your Journey

CHAPTER 8: CELEBRATING MILESTONES AND REFLECTING ON PROGRESS

Every step toward your goal reflects your effort, resilience, and growth. Celebration pays tribute to that.

Combining Celebration and Reflection

Celebration and reflection go hand in hand and together create a cycle of growth:
1. **Set a Goal:** Start with a clear, actionable goal.
2. **Take Action:** Work consistently and track your progress.
3. **Celebrate Success:** Acknowledge milestones as you achieve them.
4. **Reflect on Progress:** Identify lessons learned and areas for improvement.
5. **Refocus:** Adjust your approach and aim for the next milestone.

Tools to Track Progress

1. Progress Journals

Keep a journal to document your achievements, challenges, and reflections.

2. Milestone Charts

Create a visual representation of your journey, such as a timeline, checklist, or vision board.

3. Habit Trackers

Use apps or templates to track daily or weekly habits related to your goals.

4. Digital Tools

Apps like Trello, Notion, or Asana can help you organize tasks and milestones.

The Goal Digger's Celebration Framework
1. **Define Your Milestone:** Be clear about what success looks like for this stage of your goal.
2. **Plan Your Celebration:** Decide how you will reward yourself once you achieve it.
3. **Reflect on the Achievement:** Write down what you learned and how you feel.
4. **Share the Moment:** Celebrate with those who have supported you.
5. **Set Your Next Target:** Use the momentum to keep moving forward.

Examples of Celebrating and Reflecting

Example 1: Fitness Goal
- **Milestone:** Completing a 5K run.
- **Celebration:** Treat yourself to a massage or new workout gear.
- **Reflection:** Write about how training improved your discipline and confidence.

Example 2: Career Goal
- **Milestone:** Receiving a promotion.
- **Celebration:** Host a small dinner with close friends.
- **Reflection:** Identify the skills or actions that helped you succeed and plan to build on them.

Example 3: Personal Growth Goal
  • **Milestone:** Speaking publicly for the first time.
  • **Celebration:** Acknowledge your bravery with a self-care day.
  • **Reflection:** Note how stepping out of your comfort zone has expanded your confidence.

Final Thoughts on Celebrating and Reflecting

Every step you take toward your goals is worth celebrating. Milestones, no matter how small, represent progress, growth, and resilience. By pairing celebration with thoughtful reflection, you can maintain your motivation, refine your approach, and stay on track toward your ultimate vision.

In the next chapter, we will explore sustaining long-term success by creating a legacy that aligns with your goals and values.

10

Chapter 9: Sustaining Long-Term Success and Creating Your Legacy

Achieving short-term goals is an exhilarating experience, a testament to your dedication and hard work. However, the real test of a *Goal Digger's* resilience and commitment is sustaining long-term success. As you climb higher, you may find that the initial thrill of success wanes, and new challenges arise. The key to lasting success lies in building systems, mindsets, and habits that allow you to continue growing and thriving, regardless of obstacles.

This chapter will discuss how to sustain your progress, create a lasting impact, and ultimately leave a legacy that reflects your values, goals, and ambitions. By the end of this chapter, you will have the tools to achieve success and maintain it for years to come, creating a ripple effect that can inspire others.

The Foundation of Long-Term Success

Long-term success is not a matter of chance—it results from conscious effort, thoughtful planning, and a commitment to self-improvement. To achieve lasting success, you must build a solid foundation in key areas that keep you grounded and adaptable as you evolve.

1. Cultivating a Growth Mindset

A growth mindset is the belief that you can develop abilities and intelligence with effort, learning, and persistence. People with a growth mindset embrace challenges, learn from failure, and constantly strive to improve. Here is why a growth mindset is essential for sustaining long-term success:

• **Embrace Challenges:** Rather than avoiding difficulties, you will see them as opportunities to learn and grow.

• **Resilience:** When setbacks occur, a growth mindset helps you bounce back stronger.

• **Continuous Improvement:** You will always strive to refine your skills and knowledge, ensuring you stay relevant and competitive.

Actionable Tip: Whenever you face a challenge, ask yourself, "What can I learn from this experience?" Shift your focus from the problem to the solution and keep learning from every opportunity.

2. Creating a Personal Success System

A success system is not just a set of strategies, routines, and habits. It is your roadmap to success, your guide to navigating the challenges and opportunities that come your way. Rather than relying on sporadic bursts of motivation, your success system keeps you consistent and ensures progress over time. Key elements of a personal success system include:

• **Daily Habits:** Incorporate small, positive actions into your daily routine that build toward your bigger goals. Consistency is key, whether writing 500 words daily or setting aside time for self-reflection.

• **Time Management:** Prioritize your time based on your values and long-term objectives. Tools like time-blocking, the Pomodoro technique, or even essential to-do lists can help keep you organized.

Accountability is your secret weapon in maintaining your success system. Surround yourself with people who hold you to your commitments, whether they are mentors, friends, or accountability partners. Their support and guidance will keep you on track and ensure you are consistently moving towards your goals.

Actionable Tip: Review your current routine and identify one small habit that you can implement daily to move closer to your larger goal. Please keep the habit simple and achievable so that it becomes a sustainable part of your life.

3. Staying Adaptable

Success does not come from sticking rigidly to a single plan. It is about learning to adapt to changing circumstances and environments. The ability to pivot and adjust when necessary will help you stay on course even when obstacles arise. To maintain flexibility:

• **Monitor Trends and Changes:** Stay informed about industry trends or shifts in your personal life that may require adjustments to your goals or approach.

• **Learn from Setbacks:** Treat failure not as a defeat but as valuable feedback for improvement. Reflect on what did not work and adjust your methods.

• **Innovate:** Always look for ways to innovate and improve your processes, products, or strategies to stay ahead of the curve.

Actionable Tip: Evaluate your current path once a month. Are your strategies still effective? Do you need to make adjustments? Regular check-ins allow you to course-correct when necessary.

Building Legacy Through Consistency and Integrity

While personal success is rewarding, creating a legacy that reflects your values is even more meaningful. Your legacy is your long-lasting impact on your community, industry, and the people you touch. It is not just about what you accomplish but about how you live and your influence on others.

1. Living in Alignment with Your Values

Your actions must align with your deepest values to build a legacy of lasting significance. When your goals and actions reflect who you are at your core, they become more than just achievements- they reflect your true self, inspiring others and leaving a mark on the world.

- **Identify Your Core Values:** Reflect on what matters most, such as integrity, kindness, service, and innovation. Ensure that your personal and professional decisions align with these values.
- **Act with Integrity:** Building trust and respect is key to creating a legacy that last. Your reputation will precede you, and your actions will speak louder than words.

Actionable Tip: Make a list of your top three values. Ask yourself how your current goals and actions align with these values. Adjust your plans if necessary to ensure that you live in alignment with what you believe in.

2. Impacting Others Positively

Leaving a legacy means making a difference in others' lives. Think about how you can help others along their journey, whether by mentoring, sharing knowledge, or giving back to your community. When you help others succeed, your success becomes more meaningful.

• **Mentorship:** Share your experiences, lessons, and wisdom with those starting. Helping others achieve their goals builds a community of support.

• **Giving Back:** Find ways to give back to the causes that matter to you, such as through charity work, donations, or simply volunteering your time and skills.

Actionable Tip: Identify one person or organization you can support or mentor. Whether you help a colleague with a project or volunteer your expertise, sharing your success with others enhances your growth.

3. Building a Sustainable Business or Brand

If your goals involve creating a business, brand, or personal project, consider how it will sustain beyond your involvement. A sustainable brand or company reflects your values, culture, and vision and can thrive even when you step back.

• **Create Scalable Systems:** Focus on building replicable and efficient systems that will allow your success to continue even when you are not personally involved in every step.

• **Develop Strong Leadership:** Train and empower others to take leadership roles to ensure your vision lives on long after you.

Actionable Tip: Consider your business, brand, or personal mission without you at the helm. What systems, processes, or people need to be in place to ensure its longevity? Create a plan to build this structure.

Maintaining Work-Life Balance as You Scale

As you achieve more, you quickly become consumed by your goals. However, a key element of long-term success is maintaining balance. Your achievements will feel hollow if you neglect your well-being, relationships, and passions outside of work.

• **Prioritize Self-Care:** Take time to recharge and engage in activities that restore your energy. Balance is critical, whether exercising, traveling, reading, or spending time with loved ones.

• **Set Boundaries:** Learn to say no to opportunities or demands that do not align with your goals or values. Protect your time and energy.

Actionable Tip: Schedule time for self-care into your weekly routine. Whether it is a walk, a hobby, or a spa day, prioritize your well-being as part of your success strategy.

Building Your Legacy Over Time

Your legacy does not happen overnight; it results from a consistent, purposeful life dedicated to making a difference. Here is how you can start building it today:

1. **Clarify Your Legacy Vision:** Define what kind of impact you want to have. What do you want people to say about you when you are gone? Create a clear vision of your desired legacy.

2. **Take Action Every Day:** Every decision you make, every goal you achieve, and every person you impact contributes to your legacy.

3. **Leave a Trail of Impact:** Whether through mentorship, philanthropic work, or your achievements, focus on creating value and helping others as you go.

Actionable Tip: Write down your legacy vision. For what do you want to be remembered? What are you doing today to create that impact? Revisit this vision regularly to ensure you are on track.

Final Thoughts on Sustaining Success and Leaving a Legacy

Success is a continuous journey, and building a legacy that will last requires vision, adaptability, and an unwavering commitment to your goals and values. You can create a successful life that inspires and elevates others by focusing on consistent growth, nurturing positive relationships, and aligning with your values.

In the next section of this book, we will recap the core principles of becoming a *Goal Digger* and offer a road map for your next steps as you embark on your journey toward creating a life filled with meaning, purpose, and impact.

11

Chapter 10: The Goal Digger's Road map – Mapping Your Journey to Purposeful Success

As we have explored in previous chapters, success is not just about reaching goals; it is about building a life that aligns with your values, purpose, and vision. In this final chapter, we will take a step back, reflect on all the tools, strategies, and insights we have discussed, and create a comprehensive road map to guide your ongoing journey as a *Goal Digger*.

This road map is not a rigid, one-size-fits-all formula. It is a flexible guide that adapts to your unique path, empowering you to make it your own. Whether you are just starting or have already made significant progress, it will help you stay on track, adjust when necessary, and maintain momentum toward fulfilling your ultimate vision.

1. Start with Vision: Crafting a Purpose-Driven Life

Before you can map the road ahead, you need a clear vision of where you want to go. A vision acts as your compass, guiding your decisions and actions. The overarching purpose gives meaning to your day-to-day goals and long-term aspirations.

Create Your Vision Statement

A vision statement is a concise declaration of your life's purpose. It should encompass your dreams, values, and the impact you want to make. A well-crafted vision directs you and keeps you aligned with what truly matters.

Actionable Tip: Write a vision statement that encapsulates your goals and values. Think of it as the "big picture" of your life and career. Ask yourself questions like:
- For what do I want to be known?
- How do I want to impact others?
- What legacy do I want to leave behind?

Clarify Your Values

Your values are the guiding principles that shape your decisions and define who you are. Knowing your core values helps you stay grounded as you pursue your goals and ensures that your achievements align with your profound sense of purpose.

Actionable Tip: List your top five core values. These could include integrity, family, growth, health, or community. Use these values as a litmus test when making big decisions or setting goals. If a goal does not align with your values, consider adjusting or abandoning it.

2. Set SMART Goals: Breaking Down Your Vision into Achievable Steps

While your vision sets the direction, your goals are the concrete steps that bring you closer to your destination. To make your goals actionable and measurable, break them down using the SMART framework:
- **S**pecific: Clearly define what you want to accomplish.
- **M**easurable: Determine how you will track progress and know when you have achieved it.
- **A**chievable: Ensure that the goal is realistic and within your control.
- **R**elevant: Align your goal with your larger purpose and values.
- **T**ime-Bound: Set a deadline or timeline to maintain focus and motivation.

Actionable Tip: Apply the SMART framework to each goal. For example, instead of saying, "I want to be healthier," a SMART goal might be, "I will exercise for 30 minutes five days a week for the next three months."

3. Develop Daily Habits and Routines: The Secret to Consistency

Success does not happen overnight; it is built on consistent action. Your daily habits and routines are the foundation of your long-term success. The habits you form today will determine the person you become tomorrow.

Design a Success-Oriented Routine

Your daily routine should reflect your priorities. Allocate time for personal growth, goal-related tasks, self-care, and reflection. Consistency is key, so create habits that fit into your lifestyle and feel sustainable over time.

Actionable Tip: Identify the top three habits that will bring you closer to your goals. For example, if you aim to write a book, a daily habit might be writing for 30 minutes each morning. Make these habits a non-negotiable part of your day.

Tracking Your Progress

Tracking progress keeps you accountable and motivated. It also helps you adjust your approach if necessary. Whether you use a physical planner, an app, or a journal, find a system that works for you.

Actionable Tip: Monitor your daily progress using a habit tracker or goal-setting app (like Habitica, Trello, or Notion). Celebrate small wins as you tick off each step and adjust as needed.

4. Cultivate a Growth Mindset: Transforming Challenges into Opportunities

To achieve long-term success, you must embrace growth as a continuous process. This is what we call a 'growth mindset'. A growth mindset is the belief that your abilities and intelligence can be developed over time through hard work, learning, and perseverance. Challenges, setbacks, and failures are part of the journey and provide valuable lessons. A growth mindset is essential for navigating these obstacles without losing sight of your goals.

Embrace Setbacks as Learning Experiences

Rather than seeing failure as something negative, view it as an opportunity for learning and improvement. Each failure teaches you something new, whether a skill, mindset shift, or strategy adjustment.

Actionable Tip: When facing a setback, ask yourself, "What can I learn from this?" Use failures as stepping stones to build resilience and refine your approach.

Resilience and Perseverance

Success often requires persistence. You will encounter difficulties on the path to your dreams, but developing resilience will help you stay committed. Cultivating mental toughness and the ability to keep going when things get tough is a hallmark of successful people.

Actionable Tip: Whenever you feel discouraged, revisit your "why"—the deeper purpose behind your goals. This will renew your energy and determination to keep moving forward.

5. Surround Yourself with Support: Building a Dream Team for Shared Success

No one achieves success in isolation. Surrounding yourself with people who support your vision and push you toward your goals is essential. Through mentorship, collaboration, or friendship, a strong support network can help you overcome challenges, provide fresh perspectives, and keep you accountable.

Find Mentors and Accountability Partners

A mentor has already walked the path you want to take. They can offer guidance, advice, and wisdom to save you time and frustration.

On the other hand, an accountability partner helps you stay on track, celebrating your wins and challenging you when you veer off course.

Actionable Tip: Identify one or two people who can act as mentors or accountability partners. Schedule regular check-ins to discuss your progress and receive constructive feedback.

6. Celebrate Milestones: Staying Motivated Along the Way

As you work toward your long-term goals, remember that the journey is as important as the destination. Celebrating milestones, no matter how small, reinforces positive behavior and motivates you. Each step forward is a testament to your dedication.

Create a Celebration System

Celebrating your achievements helps you stay motivated and prevents burnout. It also allows you to reflect on how far you have come. Whether it is a small treat, a day off, or sharing your success with others, make celebration a regular part of your process.

Actionable Tip: Plan a small reward for yourself every time you hit a milestone. This could be a self-care activity, a day out with friends, or purchasing something you want. This reinforces the behavior and makes the process enjoyable.

7. Maintain Flexibility: Adjusting Your Course as You Evolve

Your goals and vision may evolve as you grow. It is essential to stay flexible and be willing to adapt your approach when necessary. Life is unpredictable, and opportunities or challenges may arise that require a change in direction.

Assess and Reevaluate Your Goals Regularly

Life circumstances change, and so will your goals. Set aside time to reevaluate your progress every few months. Ask yourself:
- Are these still the right goals for me?
- Do I need to adjust my timeline or approach?
- Have my values or priorities shifted?

Actionable Tip: Schedule regular "goal reviews" every 3-6 months. This will allow you to recalibrate and ensure you are staying true to your evolving vision.

8. Leave a Legacy: Your Long-Term Impact

As you build a successful life, think beyond the immediate. What kind of legacy do you want to leave behind? A legacy is not just about financial success—it is about how you impact others, contribute to your community, and live your values. Creating a legacy that reflects your true self is the most fulfilling part of the *Goal Digger* journey.

Define Your Legacy Vision

Your legacy is the lasting mark you leave on the world. It could be through mentorship, building a business, writing a book, or supporting a cause. Defining your legacy gives your goals deeper meaning and purpose.

Actionable Tip: Write down your legacy vision. For what do you want to be remembered? How do you want your life to inspire others? Revisit this vision regularly to ensure your actions align with the impact you want to create.

Final Thoughts: Your Ongoing Journey

Becoming a *Goal Digger* is not a destination but a lifelong journey of growth, discovery, and impact. As you implement the road map outlined in this chapter, remember that success is not linear. It is a dynamic process that requires perseverance, reflection, and an unwavering commitment to your vision.

Your journey is uniquely yours. Keep refining your goals, adapting strategies, and pursuing your dreams passionately and purposefully. The world needs your unique talents and contributions, and by following this road map, you will create a life filled with success, fulfillment, and lasting impact.

As you progress, remember that every small step is part of a more significant, meaningful path. Keep digging for your goals—because the best is yet to come.

12

Chapter 11: Embracing the Art of Goal Digger Mastery – From Success to Significance

In the previous chapters, we have explored the core elements of becoming a *Goal Digger*, from establishing clarity on your vision to creating systems for success. But as you progress, you will realize that the journey is about more than just achieving goals—it is about mastering the art of intentional living, striving for significance, and becoming someone who accomplishes things and transforms themselves and the world around them.

In this chapter, we will discuss how to elevate your goal-digging mindset from mere success to profound significance, leaving a lasting impact on your life and the lives of others. This transformation involves continuous growth, embracing new challenges, and ensuring that your goals serve a higher purpose—more than personal gain.

1. From Goal Achievement to Meaningful Impact

While accomplishing goals can be satisfying, the true essence of fulfillment lies in serving a more profound purpose beyond oneself. As a *Goal Digger*, your success should ripple outward and impact others through mentorship, innovation, social change, or inspiring the next generation.

Understanding the Shift: Success to Significance

Success is often defined by external measures: financial achievement, professional milestones, or personal accolades. However, significance is defined by the legacy you have left, the lives you have touched, and the positive changes you have inspired. To make this shift:
- **Ask the Right Questions:** Begin by asking yourself questions like:
- How can I make a difference with my success?
- What impact do I want to leave on my community, industry, or family?
- How can I contribute to causes I care about beyond my success?
- **Connect Your Goals to a Larger Purpose:** Your goals should connect to a higher purpose that transcends personal gain. Whether environmental sustainability, empowering underrepresented groups, or advocating for social justice, aligning your goals with a cause that resonates with your values will give them greater meaning.

Actionable Tip: Write down how your goals can contribute to a more significant cause. Is your business helping the environment? Is your work to mentor others? Ensuring your goals have broader implications will keep you motivated during challenging times.

2. Mastering Self-Leadership: Cultivating Inner Strength and Emotional Intelligence

To lead others effectively, you first must master self-leadership. This involves managing your thoughts, emotions, actions, and energy to help you thrive rather than burn out. It requires emotional intelligence (EQ), the ability to be aware of and control your emotions and use this awareness to guide your behavior and decisions.

Developing Emotional Intelligence

As you become more successful, you will encounter situations that require intellectual and emotional intelligence. Here is how to develop your EQ:

- **Self-awareness:** Understand your emotions and how they affect your thoughts and behavior. This awareness helps you respond thoughtfully to challenges instead of reacting impulsively.
- **Self-regulation:** Learn to manage disruptive emotions and impulses. Cultivate the ability to pause, reflect, and choose a response rather than letting emotions drive your decisions.

Empathy, the ability to understand and consider the emotions and perspectives of others, is a powerful tool for building stronger relationships and leading with compassion.

- **Social Skills:** Build strong communication and interpersonal relationships. Strong social skills are essential for effective collaboration, networking, and leadership.

Actionable Tip: Practice emotional awareness by taking time each day to reflect on your emotional state. Ask yourself, "How am I feeling today, and how does that affect my interactions and decisions?" Journaling your emotions can help develop emotional self-awareness.

Self-Discipline and Consistency

Mastering self-leadership also requires self-discipline and consistency, even when the initial motivation fades. Building habits of discipline enables you to keep moving toward your goals, even when it feels difficult.

Actionable Tip: Pick one area where you have struggled with consistency (e.g., exercise, time management, or prioritizing important work) and develop a strategy to stay disciplined. It could be as simple as scheduling specific time blocks or using tools like accountability partners or habit trackers.

3. Cultivating a Giving Mindset: Sharing Your Success

The more you achieve, the more you can give back. A *Goal-Digger* with a giving mindset is not focused solely on personal accumulation but on using their resources—time, money, knowledge, or influence—to uplift others. You build a legacy of generosity, compassion, and connection by embracing a giving mentality.

The Power of Generosity

Generosity does not just mean giving away wealth—it also means sharing your time, skills, knowledge, and influence. Giving back benefits others and enriches your life, helping you stay grounded and connected to your purpose.
  • **Mentorship and Coaching:** Share your expertise and experience with those coming up behind you. Becoming a mentor is one of the most potent ways to create a lasting impact.
  • **Community Engagement:** Get involved in your community, whether through charity work, social enterprises, or local initiatives. Your contributions do not need to be grandiose; even small acts of

service can lead to meaningful change.

Actionable Tip: Identify one person or organization you can support in the coming months. It could be through your time, knowledge, or a financial contribution. Start small but stay committed to creating a culture of giving.

4. Developing an Innovative and Creative Mindset

As a *Goal Digger,* embracing creativity and innovation is essential to staying relevant and making an impact. Success often involves solving problems in new and unique ways. The world is constantly changing, and you need to develop the mindset of an innovator who embraces change, sees opportunity in challenges, and adapts quickly.

Cultivating Creative Problem Solving

Innovation is not just about creating new products or services but about approaching problems with a fresh perspective and finding creative solutions. To be an innovative thinker:
- **Question Assumptions:** Do not accept things as they are. Challenge the status quo and think about improving processes, products, or systems.
- **Brainstorming and Collaboration:** Surround yourself with diverse thinkers and collaborate. Often, the most innovative ideas emerge from group discussions and brainstorming sessions.
- **Fail Fast, Fail Forward:** Do not be afraid to experiment. If something does not work, learn from it quickly and use that knowledge to improve. Failing forward means that when you fail, you do not just stop there; you use that failure as a stepping stone to move forward. You learn from your mistakes and apply that knowledge to your next

attempt, making it more likely to succeed.

Actionable Tip: Dedicate time each week to creative thinking. Set aside 30 minutes for brainstorming or exploring new ideas in solitude, but collaborating with others can help spark innovation.

5. Legacy Building: Creating a Lasting and Meaningful Impact

Legacy-building goes beyond financial wealth or professional success. True legacy comes from living a life that leaves a positive imprint on others. As you achieve more, think about how you can intentionally build a legacy that will live on through your actions, values, and contributions to the world.

What is a Legacy?

A legacy is not just about what you accumulate in your lifetime but your impact on others, your community, and the future. You create a legacy through the relationships you build, the values you embody, and the work you leave behind.
- **Mentoring and Teaching:** Guide others who will continue your work or carry forward your values.
- **Contributions to Society:** Identify how you can make meaningful, lasting contributions, whether through philanthropy, environmental initiatives, or systems that empower future generations.
- **Living by Example:** The most powerful legacy you can leave is through the example you set in your personal life. Be a model of integrity, resilience, and compassion.

Actionable Tip: Define what your legacy will look like. What do you want to leave behind? How you will be remembered? Start making deliberate choices that reflect the legacy you wish to create.

6. Reflecting and Evolving: The Continuous Process of Goal Digger Mastery

Mastery is not a destination but a continuous process of reflection, growth and evolution. Remember that development is ongoing as you accomplish goals and move toward your larger purpose. The *Goal-Digger* mindset is about cultivating mastery, not perfection. It is about adapting to the changes, setbacks, and lessons you encounter.

Never Stop Learning

To truly master the art of goal-digging, remain committed to lifelong learning. The more you learn, the more you evolve, and the more you can contribute. Embrace every opportunity to expand your knowledge, develop new skills, and stay curious.

• **Read Widely:** Make reading a daily habit. The more you read, the more knowledge you gain from different perspectives.

• **Attend Workshops and Seminars:** Keep sharpening your skills by attending events and courses that help you grow personally and professionally.

Actionable Tip: Focus on one new personal or professional development area over the next year. This could be a new skill, a new book topic, or a personal habit. Commit to learning and growing in that area consistently.

Final Thoughts: The Art of Becoming a Master Goal Digger

Becoming a master *Goal Digger* is about transcending personal ambition and learning to live with purpose, compassion, and integrity. By combining success with significance, creativity with discipline, and innovation with service, you elevate your journey and create a legacy to inspire and uplift others.

The path to mastery is never linear, and there will always be huddles and challenges to overcome along the journey. However, with dedication, reflection, and a commitment to continuous growth, you can live a life that leaves a lasting impact that fulfills your goals and the greater good.

As you continue your journey, remember that the process is a work of art. Keep refining, keep evolving, and, above all, keep digging for your goals. The world needs the unique contribution that only you can provide.

13

Conclusion

Conclusion: The Ongoing Journey of the Goal Digger

As we close *Goal Digger*, I want to remind you that this journey is not a destination but a lifelong process of growth, adaptation, and creation. Every step you take toward your goals builds momentum, and with each success and setback, you are refining your path to becoming the best version of yourself. Ultimately, the goal is not just to achieve but to transform: to embody the purpose, passion, and perseverance that will allow you to truly leave your mark on the world.

Being a *Goal Digger* is more than just being driven or ambitious. It is about living with intention, acting with integrity, and striving for personal and collective growth. It is about finding the courage to keep pushing forward when the road gets tough, continuously reevaluating and adjusting your goals as you evolve, and never stopping digging deeper to discover your capabilities.

The Power of Consistency and Patience

The most important thing to remember as you embark on your goal-digging journey is the power of consistency and patience. Goals are often achieved through small, incremental steps rather than giant leaps, and progress does not always resemble what we imagine. But over time, these small actions compound into something extraordinary.

Whether you are building a business, creating art, or making a difference in your community, consistent pursuit of your goals and patience will ultimately lead to lasting fulfillment. The setbacks, such as financial difficulties, creative blocks, or resistance from others, and the failures, like a project not meeting expectations or a business idea not taking off, you face along the way are merely part of the process—tools that will shape you into the person you need to be to achieve the success you desire. Here is how you can overcome them.

Actionable Tip: Whenever you feel impatient with your progress, take a moment to reflect on how far you have come. Review the milestones you have already achieved and remind yourself that the next step is approaching. Consistency is the key to long-term success. Another tip is to set specific, measurable, achievable, relevant, and time-bound (SMART) goals to keep you on track and motivated.

Aligning Your Goals with Your Values

Remember that a goal aligned with your values and purpose will feel more fulfilling than one set to achieve a certain status or acquire something material. When you start with a deep understanding of your core values, every goal you pursue will be easier to reach and more meaningful. Whether your values are growth, service, creativity, or something else, anchoring your goals in these principles creates a stronger foundation for your journey. Let your values guide your goals and inspire your journey.

Embracing Change and Adaptability

One thing is sure in life: change. As a *Goal Digger*, you will face changing circumstances, new opportunities, and unforeseen challenges. The key to thriving in an ever-changing world is adaptability. Being able to pivot when necessary, reassess your goals, and change your strategies will help you stay on course, even when things do not go as planned.

Adapting does not mean abandoning your goals; it means finding new ways to stay true to your vision, even if the path looks different than you expected. Your goals evolve as you do, and that is perfectly okay. The ability to adapt allows you to continue growing, learning, and becoming the person you were always meant to be.

Actionable Tip: Regularly reassess your goals and approach. Ask yourself: Do these goals still serve me? Have my values or circumstances shifted? Be open to change and adjust your strategies to align with your purpose.

The Importance of Self-Compassion and Reflection

It is easy to become critical of ourselves when pursuing success. We often focus too much on what has not worked rather than celebrating what we have achieved. That is why self-compassion and reflection are vital for maintaining a healthy mindset throughout your goal-digging journey. Take time to acknowledge your progress, reflect on your growth, and be kind to yourself when things are unplanned. Remember, setbacks are part of growth, not failure. Be compassionate with yourself and remember to take care of your mental and emotional well-being.

Being compassionate with yourself also means giving yourself permission to rest, recharge, and not feel guilty about taking breaks. Your journey does not require perfection—it requires presence, authenticity, and persistence.

Actionable Tip: Set aside time regularly to reflect on your wins and challenges. Take note of the lessons you have learned and the progress you have made—practice self-compassion by acknowledging that setbacks are part of growth, not failure.

A Legacy Beyond Achievement

While it is essential to set and accomplish goals, it is equally important to think about the legacy you are building along the way. True legacy comes from what you give back, how you impact others, and the difference you make in the world. Your legacy is not just about what you leave behind but also about the example you set, the lives you touch, and the changes you inspire.

When you approach your goals with this larger perspective, you create a life of significance—not just success. The world is waiting for the unique contribution only you can make. Combining your passion, skills, and purpose, you will achieve your dreams and empower others to do the same.

Final Reflection: Keep Digging for Your Goals

CONCLUSION

The *Goal-Digger* mindset is one of empowerment, focus, and resilience. It is about recognizing your power, crafting an exciting vision, and working hard to bring it to life. It is about digging deeper into your potential, staying true to your values, and continuously evolving during your journey. Remember, success is not a destination—it is a lifelong commitment to purpose, contribution and growth.

So, as you move forward, keep digging. Dig deeper into your goals, passions, potential, and the impact you can have. The tools, strategies, and mindset we have discussed are only the beginning. Your path is unique, and your capacity for greatness is limitless.

The world needs *Goal-Diggers*—people who are not only chasing their dreams but are doing so with intention, heart, and vision. And that person is you. Keep striving, growing, and digging—the best is yet to come.

With this final thought, I encourage you to start today—no matter where you are on your journey. Whether your goals are big or small, start now. The world is waiting for you to dig and unearth the incredible potential that lies within you. Keep going. The journey has just begun. And remember, self-compassion and reflection are not just tools for your journey but essential practices for a fulfilling life.

14

Resources

- Clear, J. (2018). *Atomic habits: An easy & proven way to build good habits & break bad ones.* Avery.
- Covey, S. R. (1989). *The 7 habits of highly effective people: Powerful lessons in personal change.* Free Press.
- Duckworth, A. (2016). *Grit: The power of passion and perseverance.* Scribner.
- Dolle, E. (2004). *The power of now: A guide to spiritual enlightenment.* New World Library.
- Elrod, H. (2012). *The miracle morning: The not-so-obvious secret guaranteed to transform your life (before 8AM).* Hal Elrod International, Inc.
- Dweck, C. S. (2006). *Mindset: The new psychology of success.* Ballantine Books.
- Sincero, J. (2013). *You are a badass: How to stop doubting your greatness*

- *and start living an awesome life.* Running Press.
- Peale, N. V. (1952). *The power of positive thinking.* Prentice Hall.
- Sinek, S. (2009). *Start with why: How great leaders inspire everyone to take action.* Portfolio.
- Sinek, S. (2014). *Leaders eat last: Why some teams pull together and others don't.* Portfolio.
- Brown, B. (2018). *Dare to lead: Brave work. Tough conversations. Whole hearts.* Random House.
- Canfield, J. (2005). *The success principles: How to get from where you are to where you want to be.* William Morrow.
- Ramsey, D. (2014). *The legacy journey: A radical view of your true life's purpose.* Ramsey Press.
- Cardone, G. (2011). *The 10X rule: The only difference between success and failure.* Wiley.
- Kelley, T., & Kelley, D. (2013). *Creative confidence: Unleashing the creative potential within us all.* Crown Business.
- Ries, E. (2011). *The lean startup: How today's entrepreneurs use continuous innovation to create radically successful businesses.* Crown Business.
- Brach, T. (2003). *Radical acceptance: Embracing your life with the heart of a Buddha.* Bantam.
- Brown, B. (2010). *The gifts of imperfection: Let go of who you think you're supposed to be and embrace who you are.* Hazelden Publishing.

Printed in Great Britain
by Amazon